ROBOT SPORTS

ROBOT SUMO

Tim Cooke

Lerner Publications ◆ Minneapolis

Copyright © 2025 by Lerner Publishing Group, Inc.

All rights reserved. International copyright secured. No part of this book may be reproduced, stored in a retrieval system, or transmitted in any form or by any means—electronic, mechanical, photocopying, recording, or otherwise—without the prior written permission of Lerner Publishing Group, Inc., except for the inclusion of brief quotations in an acknowledged review.

Lerner Publications Company
An imprint of Lerner Publishing Group, Inc.
241 First Avenue North
Minneapolis, MN 55401 USA

For reading levels and more information, look up this title at www.lernerbooks.com.

Main body text set in ITC Franklin Gothic.
Typeface provided by International Typeface Corporation.

Library of Congress Cataloging-in-Publication Data

Names: Cooke, Tim, 1961- author.
Title: Robot sumo / Tim Cooke.
Description: Minneapolis : Lerner Publications, [2025] | Series: Robot sports (Lerner sports) | Includes bibliographical references and index. | Audience: Ages 7-11 | Audience: Grades 2-3 | Summary: "Robot sumo matches end when one robot pushes the other out of the ring. Learn about the robots, explore the tactics, and meet the pilots and programmers who make robot sumo a high-tech contact sport"— Provided by publisher.
Identifiers: LCCN 2024017147 (print) | LCCN 2024017148 (ebook) | ISBN 9798765647950 (lib. bdg.) | ISBN 9798765662274 (pbk.) | ISBN 9798765657478 (epub)
Subjects: LCSH: Robotics—Juvenile literature. | Robot Sumo (Game)—Juvenile literature.
Classification: LCC TJ211.2 .C66 2025 (print) | LCC TJ211.2 (ebook) | DDC 629.8/92—dc23/eng/20240422

LC record available at https://lccn.loc.gov/2024017147
LC ebook record available at https://lccn.loc.gov/2024017148

TABLE OF CONTENTS

CHAPTER 1
IN THE RING 4

CHAPTER 2
READY, GO! 10

CHAPTER 3
GET CREATIVE 18

CHAPTER 4
LIFE SKILLS 24

MEET A ROBOT SUMO PLAYER 28

YOUR TURN 29

GLOSSARY 30

LEARN MORE 31

INDEX 32

CHAPTER 1

IN THE RING

Crunching metal and screeching wheels get the crowd excited. Fans watch closely as two robots clash together on a round disc. One of the machines flips the other over. It lies on its back. Can it get back up? Before it has a chance, the other robot rushes in and pushes its opponent over the edge of the disc.

Because they are designed by their builders, no two sumo robots are the same.

Fast Facts

- Sumo robots compete in different weight categories.
- Some robots have a blade at the front to help push their opponent.
- Robots are either remote-controlled or self-driven.
- A robot sumo match is won by scoring points, which are called yuhkoh.

The round has taken only five seconds! Two more rounds to go. The players reset their robots. The referee calls out to begin. Round two lasts 10 seconds. This time, the loser from round one pushes its opponent out of the ring. The game is tied.

Some robots have flags to distract their opponents.

Once a robot falls off the edge of the ring, it is defeated.

The final round begins. The two robots crash into each other. The force pushes one robot up into the air. Its opponent dashes in and pushes the upended robot out of the ring. Game over! A game of robot sumo can last for three, one-minute rounds. But sometimes it's over a lot quicker.

Robot sumo started in Japan. Hiroshi Nozawa invented the game. He led Fujisoft, a company that made robots and robot parts. He based the game on the Japanese sport sumo. In sumo, two wrestlers try to push each other out of a large ring. In robot sumo, the goal of the game is to push your opponent off a raised disc.

Sumo wrestling is a very popular sport in Japan.

Fujisoft has its headquarters in Yokohama, Japan.

Fujisoft set up the first robot sumo competition in 1989. A total of 33 robots battled. In 1998, robot sumo went international. In 2001, more than 4,000 robots entered Fujisoft's competition, which had become the World Robot Sumo Tournament.

CHAPTER 2
READY, GO!

A robot sumo match has three rounds. Winning a round gets the player one yuhkoh, or point. Two points wins the match.

Players put a lot of work into designing a successful robot.

　Players design their own sumo robots. Robots can be different in both their weight and how they are controlled. The heaviest sumo robots are controlled by a person with a handset. The handset is connected to the robot by remote control. There are two weight classes for remote-controlled robots, 6.6 pounds (2.9 kg) and 8.8 pounds (3.9 kg).

Some robots are self-driving. That means the machines control themselves. They are programmed to know how to react to the moves of their opponent. The robots use sensors to locate their opponent and to steer.

Some sumo robots are low to the ground. Others are tall.

Players cover their self-driving robots' sensors until the game is ready to begin.

The self-driving robots come in five different weights. The smallest is the nano sumo, which weighs up to 0.88 ounces (24.94 g). The largest is the mega robot sumo. It can weigh up to 6.6 pounds (3 kg).

The size of the raised disc where the game takes place depends on the weight category. The bigger the sumo, the larger the arena. The disc is flat and round, with a white border marking its edge. It is surrounded by a safety zone to protect fans from fast-moving sumo robots.

Players set up their robots on starting lines drawn on the disc.

The blade (lower right) at the front of the robot can slip beneath an opponent.

Robots begin the game by facing each other on the disc. After the referee starts the game, they crash into each other. Most robots have a blade at the front. If they get in position, they can use the blade to flip their opponent onto its back.

If a sumo robot flips over, it uses a spring or lever to turn itself upright. If the robots get stuck together, the game stops and the robots are separated. Once separated, they have five seconds to restart the game. If a robot stops moving for five seconds, their opponent wins a point.

This robot's arms are used to trick the sensors of other robots.

TECH TALK

HOW SENSORS WORK
A self-driving robot has sensors. The sensors send out a beam of light. When the light bounces off an object and returns to the sensor, the robot knows the object is there. Sumo robots have two sensors. One helps spot their opponent so they can avoid attacks. The other detects the edge of the arena.

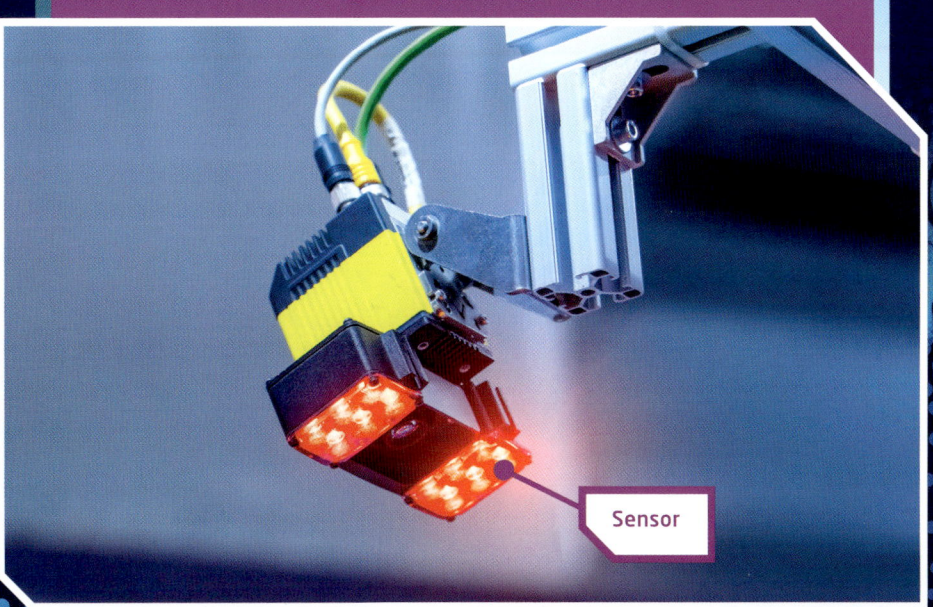

Sensor

CHAPTER 3
GET CREATIVE

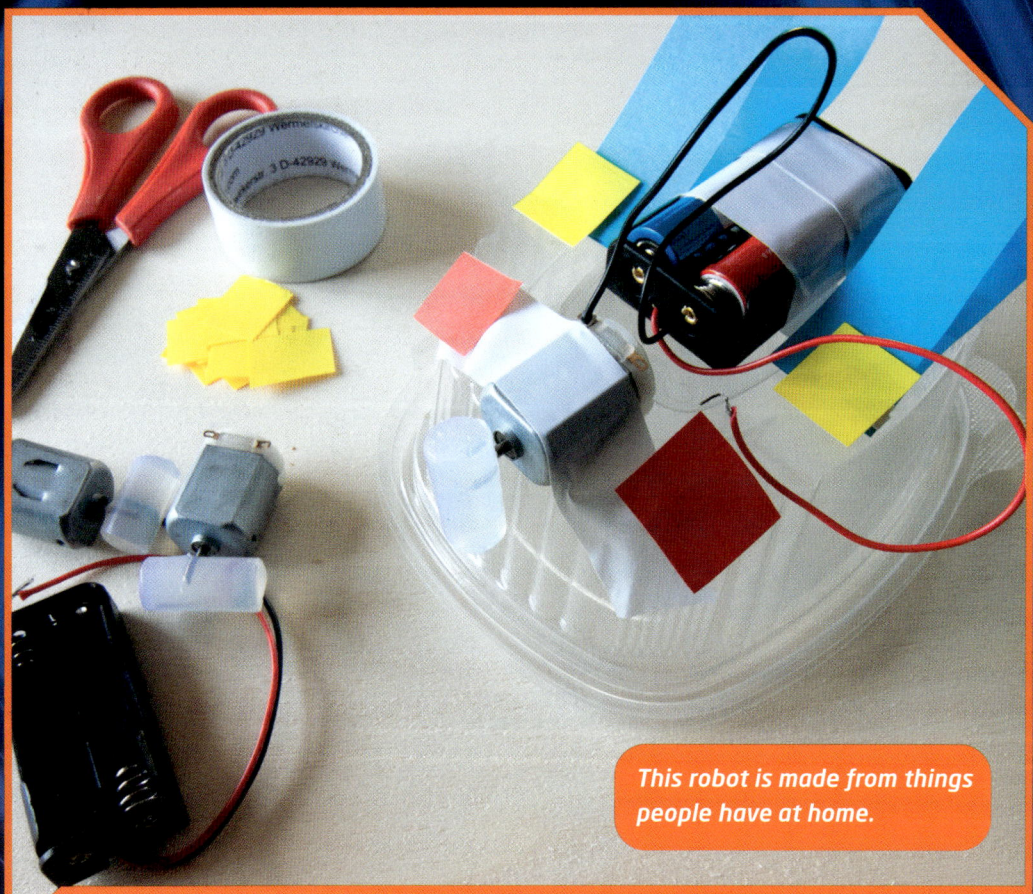

This robot is made from things people have at home.

Robot sumo is unpredictable. The biggest robot doesn't always win. Neither does the most expensive.

Two-wheeled robots are fast but can be tricky to steer.

Most players build their own sumo robots. Being creative is part of the fun. Some robots are built from pieces of metal and materials from the trash. Your bot could be low and heavy, so it is difficult to push out of the ring. Or it could be light and fast. Being small could make it easier for your opponent if it catches you.

Robots can have two, four, or six wheels. Many players prefer to use six wheels. The wheels provide grip. Having fewer wheels makes the robot harder to steer.

The body of the robot can be made from any material. But it has to be strong enough to be crashed into during a fight. Most players use a light metal, such as aluminum, or a type of plastic. Some print their robots using 3-D printers.

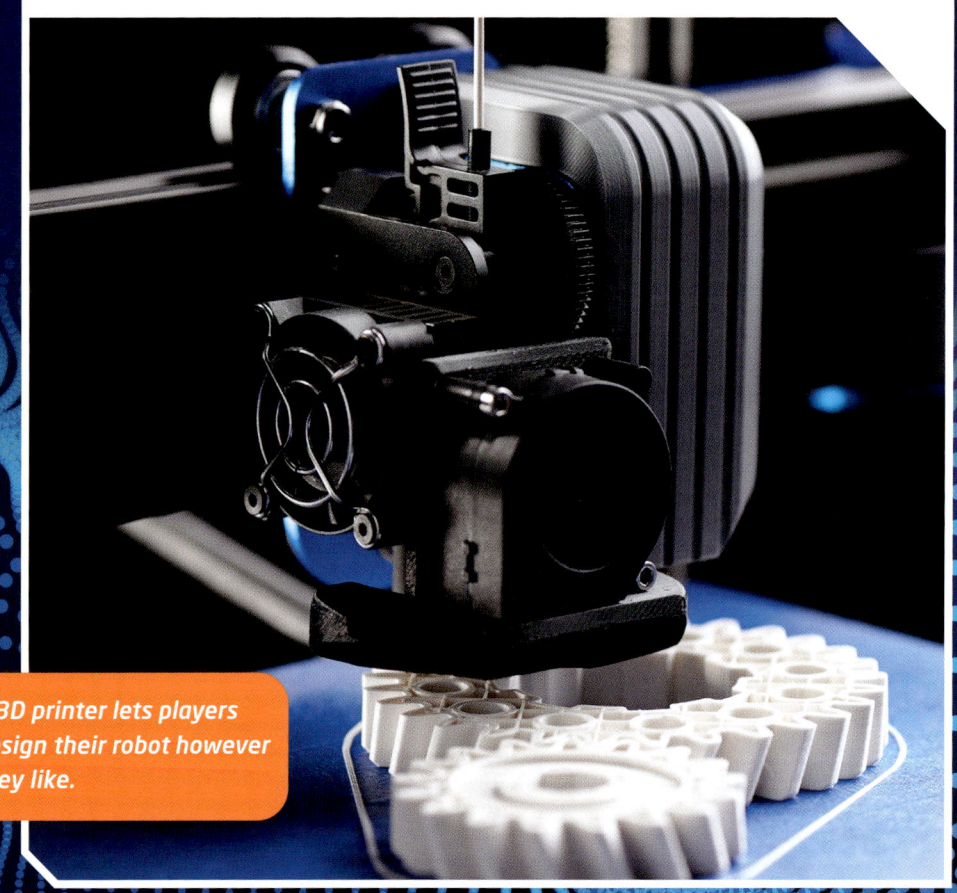

A 3D printer lets players design their robot however they like.

The microcontroller responds to information from the robot's sensors.

The body of the robot protects the motors, wires, battery, and sensors inside. The most important part of a self-driving robot is its microcontroller. The microcontroller is the robot's brain. It uses the signals from the sensors to decide how to steer the robot.

The simplest robots are glued together from cardboard and popsicle sticks. Players can add a simple microcontroller. They write code on their laptop to control the robot. Another favorite building material is plastic building blocks. The little bricks can be put together in any shape.

Pieces from building toys are easy to fit together to build a robot.

Tech Talk

DOWN FORCE

A sumo robot needs to be difficult to push around. The force that helps it stay in the arena is friction. Friction occurs when two surfaces move against each other. The more friction, the slower the movement. Robot builders add weights to make their robots heavier, which means more friction.

Friction slows a ball rolling down a slope.

CHAPTER 4
LIFE SKILLS

Robot sumo players learn how to build, program, and control their robots. These are the skills they need to become a champion in the arena. They are also great skills to have for future STEM careers.

Robots are used in factories to build machines such as cars.

Robots make work a lot easier in jobs that require precise movements, such as fitting tiny pieces of a toy together. They also work in environments that are dangerous for people, such as extreme heat. Flying robots, called drones, can be used to make deliveries, and medical robots can help with surgery. Some robots can even help prepare food.

The coding skills players learn can be useful in a wide range of careers.

As the use of robots grows, we will need more experts to design and operate them. The skills that students learn from designing sumo robots will help them understand how to create helpful machines. That is one reason robot sumo continues to grow. Schools understand that it is a great introduction to STEM skills.

Maybe you could take your own robot all the way to the Robot Sumo World Competition? You might even become the champion!

TECH TALK

CODING
Players instruct sumo robots using code. Code is written as a list of text instructions. The instructions are then turned into a language the microcontroller can understand. The code tells the robot what to do if it detects its opponent. It also tells it how to steer away from the edge of the disc.

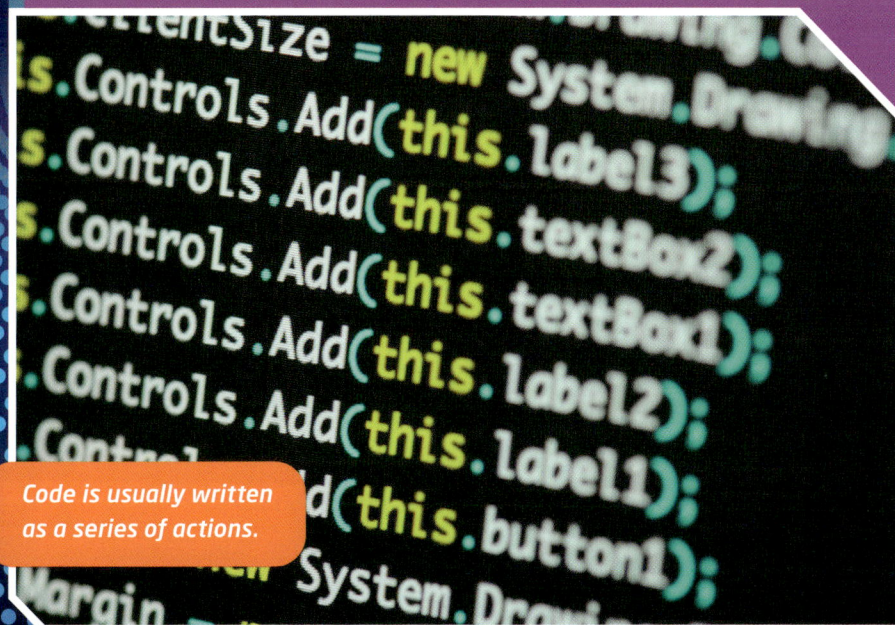

Code is usually written as a series of actions.

MEET A ROBOT SUMO PLAYER

Oran Duignan entered his first robot sumo tournament as part of a college project. He and his teammates had 12 weeks to build a sumo robot. Oran did the coding. His teammates thought about how to design and build the robot.

After six weeks, the team faced their first competition. The robot's task was to find an object in the arena. The robot was very slow.

Oran realized that there were errors in his codes. Once the codes were fixed, the robot got better at locating other objects.

In the final tournament, the robot won two out of its four fights. Oran's team climbed up the league—and they started looking forward to the next robot sumo challenge!

YOUR TURN

Now that you know more about robot sumo, it's time for you to get involved. The good news is anyone can do it. Here are some tips.

- Ask your school if you can try to get robot kits for free. Toy companies sometimes supply free equipment to school groups.

- Start an after-school club with your friends. That way you can help one another solve problems and build the best robot. Ask teachers who might be interested in helping you.

- If you want to try building a robot at home, start with simple materials.

- Check for robot sumo events that can be viewed on TV or streamed online.

Glossary

arena: a large area used for sports or entertainment

friction: the force that slows down objects when they rub against each other

handset: a device that sends signals to a robot

microcontroller: a simple computer that controls a machine

opponent: the person you play against in a contest

program: to instruct a computer how to act

remote control: the control of operating a machine from a distance

robot: a machine that can be programmed to perform actions

sensor: a device that measures changes

STEM: short for science, technology, engineering, math

Learn More

Farrell, Jessica. *How to Build LEGO Robots.* New York: DK Children, 2024.

Fujisoft All Japan Robot-Sumo Tournament, Introduction to Robot Sumo
https://www.fsi.co.jp/sumo/robot/en/about.html

Katovich, Bob. *Awesome Robotics Projects for Kids.* Emeryville, CA: Rockridge Press, 2019.

Rea, Amy C. *Robot and Drone Technology.* Parker, CO: The Child's World, 2023.

Robogames, Robot Sumo rules
https://robogames.net/rules/all-sumo.php

Sphero, How to Build a Robot
https://sphero.com/blogs/news/how-to-build-a-robot

INDEX

arena, 14, 17, 23, 24, 28

code, 22, 27, 28

friction, 23

Fujisoft, 8-9

Japan, 8-9

Nozawa, Hiroshi, 8

sensor, 12-13, 16-17, 21

skills, 24, 26

Sumo wrestling, 8

wheels, 4, 19

PHOTO ACKNOWLEDGMENTS

Image credits: Aflo/Shutterstock, pp. 4, 6-7, 10, 12, 24; Lisi Niesner/EPA/Shutterstock, pp. 5, 13, 14; J. Henning Buchholz/Shutterstock, p. 8; Fujisoft/Wikimedia Commons, p. 9; noxphotos.com/Shutterstock, pp. 11, 15-16, 21-22, 29; asharkyu/Shutterstock, p. 17; Paolo De Gasperis/Dreamstime.com, p. 18; RaspberryStudio/ Shutterstock, p. 19; R_Boe/Shutterstock, p. 20; MilanB/Shutterstock, p. 23; Jenson/Shutterstock, p. 25; Alex006007/Shutterstock, p. 26; Casimiro PT/Shutterstock, p. 27. Design elements: Rendix Alextian/Shutterstock, pp. 1, 3, 4, 12, 18, 24; Stocklekkies/Shutterstock, pp. 5-11, 13-17, 19-23, 25-32.

Cover credits: Rendix Alextian/Shutterstock (top); Katie Nesling/Dreamstime.com (top, left); Ieva Babre/Dreamstime.com (top, right); World Intellectual Property Organization (WIPO)/Wikimedia Commons (bottom).